A Primary Source Guide to

KENYA

Janey Levy

ROSEN CLASSROOM
PRIMARYSOURCE

Rosen Classroom Books & Materials

New York

Published in 2003 by The Rosen Publishing Group, Inc.
29 East 21st Street, New York, NY 10010

Book Design: Haley Wilson

Photo Credits: Cover, p. 1 © Anup Shah/FPG International; p. 4 (map) © Map Resource; p. 4 (inset) © Dave G. Houser/Corbis; pp. 5, 6, 14, 18, 19 © Carl & Ann Purcell/Corbis; p. 8 © AP Wide World Photos; p. 10 © Bettmann/Corbis; p 11 © Gilbert Liz/Corbis Sygma; p. 12 © Michael S. Lewis/Corbis; p. 16 © Adrian Arbib/Corbis; p. 20 © Yann Arthus-Bertrand/Corbis; p. 21 © Vittonano Rastelli/Corbis; p. 22 © Jan Butchofsky-Houser/Corbis.

Library of Congress Cataloging-in-Publication Data

Levy, Janey.
  A primary source guide to Kenya / Janey Levy.
       p. cm.
Summary: Text and photographs reveal the culture, history, artifacts, and traditions of the African nation, Kenya.
  ISBN 0-8239-6590-2 (library binding)
  ISBN 0-8239-8074-X (pbk.)
  6-pack ISBN: 0-8239-8081-2
  1. Kenya—Juvenile literature. [1. Kenya.] I. Title.
  DT433.522 .L48 2003
  967.62—dc21

                              2002004163

Manufactured in the United States of America

Contents

L. Chad

YEMEN

SUDAN

ETHIOPIA

SOMALIA

UGANDA

KENYA

Congo

Lake
Victoria

Nairobi

Mombasa

TANZANIA

Indian
Ocean

L. Malawi

A Look at Kenya

Kenya lies along the **equator** in eastern Africa. It is about twice the size of the state of Nevada. Kenya's coastline borders the Indian Ocean and is about 330 miles (531 kilometers) long.

Some of the first humans on Earth lived in Kenya millions of years ago. Like those early people, more than three-quarters of Kenya's people still live in the countryside. Today, Kenya is famous for its coffee and also for its wildlife, which draws visitors from all over the world.

◀ The capital of Kenya is Nairobi. Mombasa is the country's most important port.

The Land

Kenya has three types of land. One type of land is coastland, with its beautiful beaches and rain forests. The coast receives about forty inches (102 centimeters) of rainfall each year.

West of the coast are the plains, which cover most of Kenya. The plains get very little rain, and few plants can grow there. **Nomads** in this area move often, looking for food for their cattle.

The **highland** is in southwestern Kenya. Most of Kenya's farms are in the highland because it has rich soil that is good for growing crops. Most of Kenya's people live there.

◀ Mount Kenya is the second tallest mountain in Africa. It is more than three miles (five kilometers) high!

Kenya's History

The first Kenyans lived more than 2 million years ago! About 3,000 years ago, the **ancestors** of today's Kenyans arrived from other parts of Africa.

About 700 A.D., Arabs began settling along Kenya's coast. They controlled the area until Portuguese settlers arrived around 1500. In the late 1600s, Arabs took control of the coast again.

English rule began around 1895. Kenyans had no voice in the government. The suffering of many Kenyans led to a **revolt** against English rule in the 1940s. Kenyans fought against the English throughout the 1950s. In 1963, Kenya won its independence.

◀ The Kenyan soldier in this picture is lowering the British flag at Uhuru Stadium in Nairobi on December 11, 1963. This photograph appeared on the front page of the *New York Times* on December 12, 1963. The map also shown here is from the same article.

The Government of Kenya

The government that was created for independent Kenya is much like the government of the United States. Kenya is a **republic**, with a **constitution** that grants people rights such as the freedom to say what they think.

Kenya's leader is a president who is elected by the people. Like the United States Congress, Kenya's

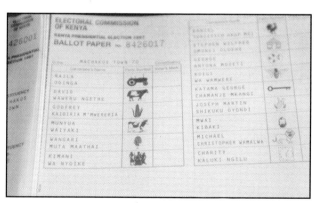

National **Assembly** makes laws for the country. Assembly members are chosen by the voters and the president.

◀ Kenya's first president was Jomo Kenyatta. This photo shows Kenyatta surrounded by supporters just after he was elected president in 1963. He is waving a fly wisk, which is a symbol of authority in Kenya. Pictured above is a ballot from the 1997 presidential elections in Kenya.

11

Coffee, Tea, and Tourists

Coffee and tea are the most important crops grown in Kenya. They are sold all over the world and bring more money to Kenya than anything else. Thousands of Kenyans work on the large farms, or **plantations**, where coffee and tea are grown.

Tourists also bring a lot of money to Kenya. More than half a million tourists visit Kenya each year. Some come to enjoy the beaches. Many more come to see the wildlife.

◀ Harvesting tea is hard work. Harvesters pick the tea leaves by hand and put them in large baskets they carry on their backs. The 100-shilling banknote and coins above bear the image of Daniel T. arap Moi, who became president in 1978.

13

Kenya's People

The Kikuyu are Kenya's largest **ethnic** group. Most Kikuyu and other groups live in small villages. Some groups, like the Maasai, are nomads who raise cattle. Each group has its own language, although most know Kiswahili. Educated people also know English, Kenya's official language.

Most Kenyans are Christians. There are also many Muslims in Kenya. Many Kenyans still hold ancient beliefs. The Maasai believe that God gave them cattle and no one else has the right to own cattle. The Kikuyu believe that God lives on Mount Kenya when he visits Earth.

◀ The Kikuyu are farmers who live in small houses made of mud or branches, with dirt floors and grass roofs.

The Importance of Kinship

Kinship is a powerful force for Kenyans. They believe that people exist only as part of the group, not as separate individuals. Kinship binds together everyone in a village, even people who have left to live somewhere else. It even includes everyone who lived before and everyone yet to be born. Kinship also includes animals, plants, and objects.

Kenyans consider visitors to be part of the community and welcome them with tea and food. Kenyans always make more food than they need, so they will have enough for unexpected visitors.

◀ One common food in Kenya is soup made from groundnuts, or peanuts. It is served in bowls made from gourds.

The Arts

Dance is one of the most important Kenyan art forms. Village **ceremonies** for births, marriages, deaths, and other events include dancing. Dancers often wear special clothes and **jewelry**. They also paint their bodies.

Making beautiful cloth is another Kenyan art form. Kenyan women usually wear a colorful cloth called a *kanga* over their other clothing. *Kangas*

have Kiswahili sayings on them, such as "Don't remember only the bad things and forget to be thankful for the good things."

The Maasai are famous for their brightly colored beaded jewelry.

◀ The photo on the opposite page shows women and men performing a traditional Kikuyu dance.

19

Today, Kenyans are working hard to solve their country's problems. They want to end the suffering of Kenyans who don't have good houses or enough food. They want to get rid of pollution, which has made water unsafe to drink. Kenyans know they can solve these problems only by working together. "*Harambee*," the Kiswahili word for "working together," is on the nation's **coat of arms** as a reminder.

◀ The port city of Mombasa is one of the largest manufacturing centers in Kenya. Wastes from factories can put sea life in danger.

Kenya at a Glance

Population: About 30 million

Capital: Nairobi

Largest City: Nairobi (population about 1 million)

Official Name: Republic of Kenya

National Anthem: "Wimbo Wa Taifa" ("National Anthem")

Land Area: 224,081 square miles (580,367 square kilometers)

Government: Republic

Unit of Money: Kenya shilling

Flag: Black stands for Kenya's people, red for the blood spilled in the struggle for freedom, and green for Kenya's crops. The shield and spears stand for guarding liberty.

Glossary

ancestor (AN-ses-tuhr) Someone in your family who lived before you.

assembly (uh-SEM-blee) A group of leaders elected by the people to make laws for a country.

ceremony (SEHR-uh-moh-nee) An event in honor of something important.

coat of arms (KOAT UV ARMS) A shield shape with blocks of color and pictures. It stands for a country or a person.

constitution (kon-stuh-TOO-shun) A set of rules for a government.

equator (ih-KWAY-tuhr) An imaginary line around the middle of Earth that separates it into two parts, north and south.

ethnic (ETH-nick) Relating to a group of people who have the same race, nationality, beliefs, and ways of living.

highland (HI-luhnd) An area with many mountains.

jewelry (JOO-uhl-ree) Objects made of gold, silver, pretty stones, or beads that people wear for decoration.

kinship (KIN-ship) The condition of being part of a family or very close community.

nomad (NOH-mad) Someone who moves around all the time and does not have a fixed home.

plantation (plan-TAY-shun) A large farm owned by one family and worked by many people.

republic (ruh-PUH-blick) A type of government in which laws are made by leaders elected by the people.

revolt (rih-VOLT) A war to overthrow a government.

tourist (TOOR-ist) Someone who travels for pleasure to see new places or learn new things.

Index

Primary Source List

Page 5. Sign marking equator on the road to Mount Kenya in Nanyuki, Kenya.
Page 8. Kenyan soldier lowering British flag. Photograph taken December 11, 1963, in Nairobi.
Page 8 (inset). "Joyful Kenya Attains Independence From Britain." *New York Times*, December 12, 1963. Page 18.
Page 10. Jomo Kenyatta. Photograph taken May 8, 1963, in Nairobi.
Page 11. Ballot for presidential elections in Kenya, 1997.
Page 13. Kenyan 100-shilling banknote and coins.
Page 14. Kikuyu village and farmland. Photograph by Carl Purcell in the early 1980s.
Page 16. Maasai woman cooking inside a house. Photograph by Adrian Arbib in the Loita Hills of southern Kenya between 1970 and 1994.
Page 18. Painted Kikuyu dancers. Photograph by Carl Purcell in the early 1980s in Outspan, Kenya.
Page 19. Maasai beaded necklaces. Photograph by Carl Purcell in the mid-1980s.
Page 21. Official coat of arms. Photograph by Vittoriano Rastelli in Nairobi in May 1980.

Web Sites

Due to the changing nature of Internet links, The Rosen Publishing Group, Inc. has developed an on-line list of Web sites related to the subjects of this book. This site is updated regularly. Please use this link to access the list:
http://www.powerkidslinks.com/pswc/pske/